Franz
LISZT

Von der Wiege bis zum Grabe

Symphonic Poem No. 13
S. 107

Study Score
Partitur

PETRUCCI LIBRARY PRESS

INTRODUCTION

The present score is a reissue of one from the Franz Liszt-Stiftung edition, originally published by Breitkopf & Härtel from 1907-1936. The edition was prepared in an effort to publish the entire oeuvre of Franz Liszt. Editors included such prominent musicians as Béla Bartok, Ferruccio Busoni, Eugène d'Albert and José Vianna da Motta – some of whom studied with Liszt – as well as scholars like Peter Raabe, who would later compile the first catalog of the composer's works. The need for a complete edition was already apparent by the time of Liszt's death. Although some of his piano music had regularly appeared in new editions throughout his life, these works were by no means representative of even his pianistic output. A far more unfortunate fate was left for his orchestral music - which would usually be issued only once, soon to go out of print and later scarcely available. The Liszt-Stiftung edition revived many works that had fallen into relative obscurity and was therefore handsomely welcomed.

The edition was sadly never completed. The publication activity was brought to a premature end by the time of the Second World War. All in all the incomplete edition encompassed 34 volumes, among others two symphonies, the symphonic poems, some concert works, a couple of piano arrangements and 11 volumes of original works for piano – a mere fraction of the composer's output – but the edition would nonetheless break the ground for Liszt research during the 20th century for a number of reasons. First, it brought to light a number of late pieces that would put Liszt as a forerunner of experimental music and firmly establish his position as such. Second, it revealed the diversity of Liszt's output, which up until that time had been best known as an important addition to the piano repertoire. Third, it displayed the complex and characteristic nature of many of his works by being the first edition to show and make use of several alternative (sometimes vastly different) versions and sources. Last but not least, it would provide the world with a generally reliable edition of easy availability and very high standard for its day.

The Bavarian State Library acquired a complete copy of said edition and decided to digitize it in 2008. By that time more than 70 years had passed since its publication, effectively rendering the edition out of copyright and free for any use. Each and every page was scanned and uploaded to their online digital collection. While this was a great effort in itself, the site has a rudimentary interface, is difficult to navigate and the scores are not in the context of relevant information. One of our users decided to also upload it to our site, the International Music Score Library Project (IMSLP) / Petrucci Music Library, the unique wiki-based repository of musical scores, composers and indexes that anyone can edit and amend. Through the effort of a single user, Mattias K. (piupianissimo), the entire edition is now easily available worldwide to those who wish to perform and study the composer's music in a historical context, since as the case is with Liszt's music, many early editions exist and many are readily available on the site and many more will be available in the future. IMSLP is as such a valuable resource available to the scholar but even more to the performer who is always a mere mouse click away from scores that have not been in print since the turn of the past century, or that are otherwise hard to come by. The availability, quantity of ease of access for online scores will soon exceed those of the traditional medium of print. Nevertheless new works have always been published through the printed medium and this tradition is going to persist for many years to come even if complemented by the digital medium. Of course an important fact to stress is that the availability of digital scores online does not exclude the need of printed score since neither one can replace the comfort and neatness of one another. The quality of a bound reprint or new engraving exceeds that of a score printed at home.

I discovered IMSLP back in early 2006 when it first began. At that time many scores were scattered on the net either privately or on commercial collection sites. Many of these sites had a considerably large collection but sadly many had restrictions on number of downloads per day and the process of contributing to them was riddled with bureaucracy. IMSLP was the first free site where anyone could contribute and upload any kind of musical scores. I have personally searched and uploaded many works – particularly those of Liszt – and the future of the site is nothing but bright. At the time of its start only a handful of scores were available on the site but through the effort of its users IMSLP has grown to be the largest collection of scores available on the Internet.

Von der Wiege bis zum Grabe is the final work in a series of thirteen symphonic poems composed by Franz Liszt. It was composed from 1881-82 and first published in 1883 by Bote und Bock of Berlin. The dedicatee is Count Géza Zichy. This score is from the twelfth volume of the Franz Liszt-Stiftung edition, edited by Berthold Kellermann and published in 1913. The score, along with a number or arrangements, is also available directly at the following URL:
http:// imslp.org/wiki/Von_der_Wiege_bis_zum_Grabe,_S.107_(Liszt,_Franz)

Soren Afshar (Funper)

Summer, 2011

COMPOSER'S PREFACE

Eine Aufführung, welche den Intentionen des Komponisten entsprechen und ihnen Klang, Farbe, Rhythmus und Leben verleihen soll, wird bei meinen Orchester-Werken am zweckmässigsten und mit dem geringsten Zeitverlust durch geteilte Vor-Proben gefördert werden. Demzufolge erlaube ich mir, die HH. Dirigenten, welche meine symphonischen Dichtungen aufzuführen beabsichtigen, zu ersuchen, der General-Probe Separat-Proben mit dem Streich-Quartett, andere mit Blas- und Schlag-Instrumenten vorangehen zu lassen.

Gleichzeitig sei mir gestattet zu bemerken, dass ich das mechanische, taktmässige, zerschnittene Auf- und Abspielen, wie es an manchen Orten noch üblich ist, möglichst beseitigt wünsche, und nur den periodischen Vortrag, mit dem Hervortreten der besonderen Accente und der Abrundung der melodischen und rhythmischen Nuanzierung, als sachgemäss anerkennen kann. In der geistigen Auffassung des Dirigenten liegt der Lebensnerv einer symphonischen Produktion, vorausgesetzt, dass im Orchester die geziemenden Mittel zu deren Verwirklichung sich vorfinden; andernfalls möchte es ratsamer erscheinen, sich nicht mit Werken zu befassen, welche keineswegs eine Alltags-Popularität beanspruchen.

Obschon ich bemüht war, durch genaue Anzeichnungen meine Intentionen zu verdeutlichen, so verhehle ich doch nicht, dass Manches, ja sogar das Wesentlichste, sich nicht zu Papier bringen lässt, und nur durch das künstlerische Vermögen, durch sympathisch schwungvolles Reproduzieren, sowohl des Dirigenten als der Aufführenden, zur durchgreifenden Wirkung gelangen kann. Dem Wohlwollen meiner Kunstgenossen sei es daher überlassen, das Meiste und Vorzüglichste an meinen Werken zu vollbringen.
Weimar, März 1856.

Pour obtenir un résultat d'exécution correspondant aux intentions de mes œuvres orchestrales, et leur donner le coloris, le rhythme, l'accent et la vie qu'elles réclament, il sera utile d'en préparer la répétition générale par des répétitions partielles des instruments à cordes, à vent, en cuivre, et à percussion. Par cette méthode de la division du travail on épargnera du temps en facilitant aux exécutants l'intelligence de l'ouvrage. Je me permets en conséquence de prier MM. les chefs d'orchestre qui seraient disposés à faire exécuter l'un de ces Poèmes symphoniques, de vouloir bien prendre le soin de faire précéder les répétitions générales, des répétitions préalables indiquées ci-dessus.

En même temps j'observerai que la mesure dans les œuvres de ce genre demande à être maniée avec plus de mesure, de souplesse, et d'intelligence des effets de coloris, de rhythme, et d'expression qu'il n'est encore d'usage dans beaucoup d'orchestres. Il ne suffit pas qu'une composition soit régulièrement bâtonnée et machinalement exécutée avec plus ou moins de correction pour que l'auteur ait à se louer de cette façon de propagation de son œuvre, et puisse y reconnaître une fidèle interprétation de sa pensée. Le nerf vital d'une belle exécution symphonique gît principalement dans la compréhension de l'œuvre reproduite, que le chef d'orchestre doit surtout posséder et communiquer, dans la manière de partager et d'accentuer les périodes, d'accuser les contrastes tout en ménageant les transitions de veiller tantôt à établir l'équilibre entre les divers instruments, tantôt à les faire ressortir soit isolément soit par groupes, car à tel moment il convient d'entonner ou de marquer simplement les notes, mais à d'autres il s'agit de phraser, de chanter, et même de déclamer. C'est au chef qu'il appartient d'indiquer à chacun des membres de l'orchestre la signification du rôle qu'il a à remplir.

Je me suis attaché à rendre mes intentions par rapport aux nuances, à l'accélération et au retard des mouvements, etc. aussi sensibles que possible par un emploi détaillé des signes et des expressions usitées; néanmoins ce serait une illusion de croire qu'on puisse fixer sur le papier ce qui fait la beauté et le caractère de l'exécution. Le talent et l'inspiration des artistes dirigeants et exécutants en ont seuls le secret, et la part de sympathie que ceux-ci voudront bien accorder à mes œuvres, seront pour elles le meilleur gage de succès.
Weimar, Mars 1856.

In order to secure a performance of my orchestral works which accords with their intentions, and which imparts to them the colour, rhythm, accent and life that they require, it is recommended that the general rehearsal should be preceded by separate rehearsals of the Strings, Wind, Brass, and instruments of percussion. By this division of labour time will be saved, and the executants will more rapidly be made familiar with what is required of them. I therefore venture to request that conductors, who are pleased to bring one or the other of my symphonic poems to a hearing will adopt the plan formulated above.

At the same time I may be allowed to remark that it is my wish that the mechanical, bar by bar, up and down beating of time, which obtains in so many places, should as far as possible be discarded, and that only the periodic divisions, with the prominence of certain accentuation and the rounding off of melodic and rhythmical nuances should alone be regarded as indispensable. The vitality of a symphonic performance depends upon the intellectual perception of the conductor, presuming that suitable material for its realisation is to be found in the orchestra; failing this it would seem to be advisable to hold aloof from works which do not claim a promise of every-day popularity.

Although I have endeavoured to make my intentions clear by providing exact marks of expression, I cannot conceal from myself that much, and that perhaps the most important, cannot be set forth on paper, but can only be successfully brought to light by the artistic capability and the sympathetic and enthusiastic reproduction by both conductor and executants. It may therefore be left to my colleagues in art to do the most and best that they can for my works.
Weimar, March 1856.

F. Liszt.

After the 1854 relief by Ernst Rietschel

INSTRUMENTATION

2 Flutes

Piccolo

3 Oboes

(3rd also English Horn)

2 Clarinets

2 Bassoons

4 Horns

2 Trumpets

3 Trombones

Tuba

Timpani

Cymbals

Harp

Violins I

Violins II

Violas

Violoncellos

Basses

Duration: ca. 13 minutes

First Performance: 1927

ISBN: 978-1-60874-038-3

This score is an unabridged reprint of the score
first issued in Leipzig by Breitkopf & Härtel, 1913. Plate F.L. 18

Printed in the USA
First Printing: December, 2011

Michael von Zichy verehrungsvoll gewidmet

VON DER WIEGE BIS ZUM GRABE

Symphonic Poem No. 13

S. 107

FRANZ LISZT (1811–1886)

I.

Die Wiege. The cradle. Le berceau.
A bölcső.

dim.
sempre p
sempre p
sempre p
un poco rall.
a tempo
dolce
mp
sempre arpeggiando
sempre dolce
sempre dolce
sempre dolce
un poco rall.
a tempo
sempre legato

non troppo p
un poco marc.
sempre dolciss.
sempre dolciss. e legato
sempre dolciss. e legato
sempre legato
legato
sempre legato
sempre legato

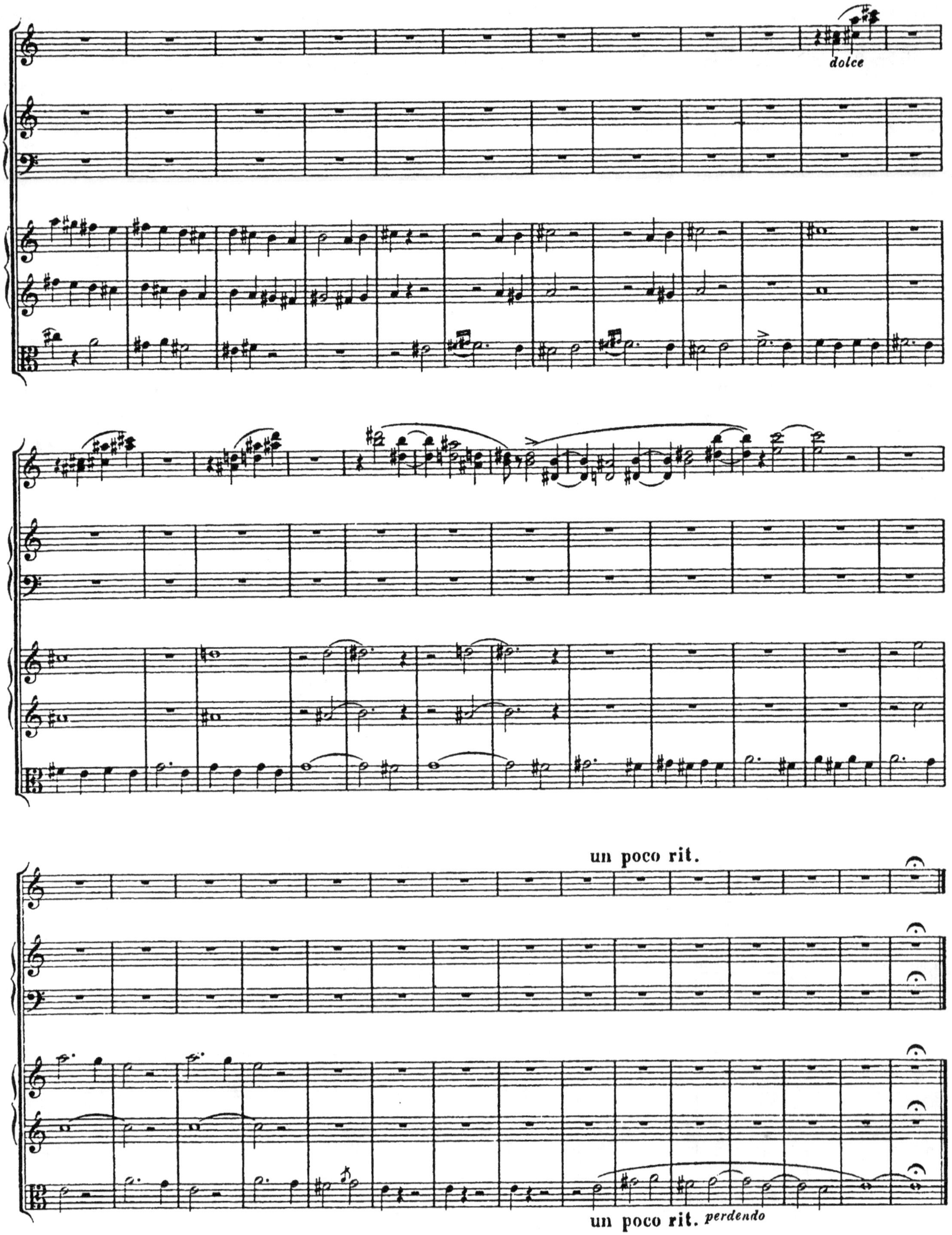
dolce
un poco rit.
un poco rit. perdendo

II.
Der Kampf um's Dasein.
The struggle for existence.   Le combat pour la vie.
Küzdelem a létért.

Fl.
a 2
p
Hob.
a 2
p
Fag.
mf
1. u. 2. Hr.
p
p
p
p
mf marc.
mf marc.
Hob.
mf nobilmente
Klar.
mf nobilmente cantando
mf nobilmente cantando
Fag.
1. u. 2. Hr.
a 2
mf
mf nobilmente
mf nobilmente
div.
mf nobilmente
p
p

Fl.
a 2
mf poco a poco cresc.
Hob.
poco a poco cresc.
Klar.
poco a poco cresc.
Fag.
poco a poco cresc.
1. u. 2. Hr.
poco a poco cresc.
poco a poco cresc.
poco a poco cresc.
poco a poco cresc.
poco a poco cresc.
poco a poco cresc.
Fl. a 2
Hob.
Klar.
Fag.
cresc.
a 2
f marc.
Hr.
f marc.
3. Pos. u. Tuba.
p
B
cresc.
cresc.

1. u. 2. Hr.
ff
ff violente
ff violente
ff violente
Vcl. u. Kb.
1. u. 2. Hr.
p
sempre ff
sempre ff
sempre ff
div.
Vcl.
ff
Kb.
mf
mf
Fl.
a 2
p
Hob.
a 2
p
Fag.
mf
1. u. 2. Hr.

40338

a 2
Fl.
Hob.
Klar.
Fag.
Hr.
3. Pos. u. Tuba.
f ma non troppo
sempre legato
f ma non troppo
sempre legato
f ma non troppo
sempre legato
a 2
f ma non troppo
f marc. sempre
a 2
f marc. sempre
f ma non troppo
f ma non troppo
f ma non troppo
f marc. sempre
f marc. sempre
a 2
Fl.
Hob.
Klar.
Fag.
a 2
a 2
Hr.
a 2
cresc.

Kl. Fl.
f cresc.
Fl.
Hob.
Klar.
Fag.
a 2
Hr.
Tr.
1. u. 2. Pos.
3. Pos. u. Tuba.
Pk.
f marc.
Bck.

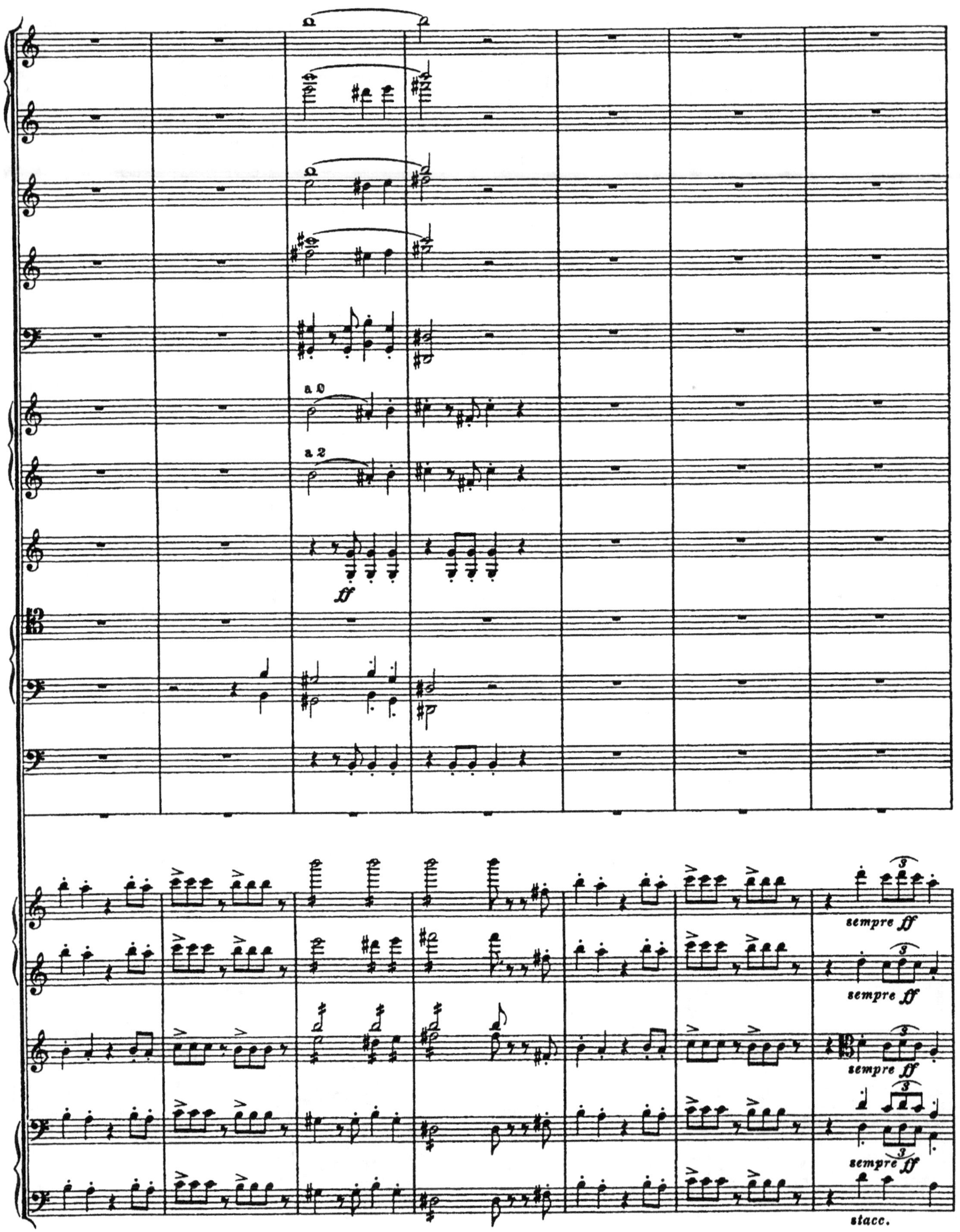
a 2
a 2
ff
sempre ff
sempre ff
sempre ff
sempre ff
stacc.

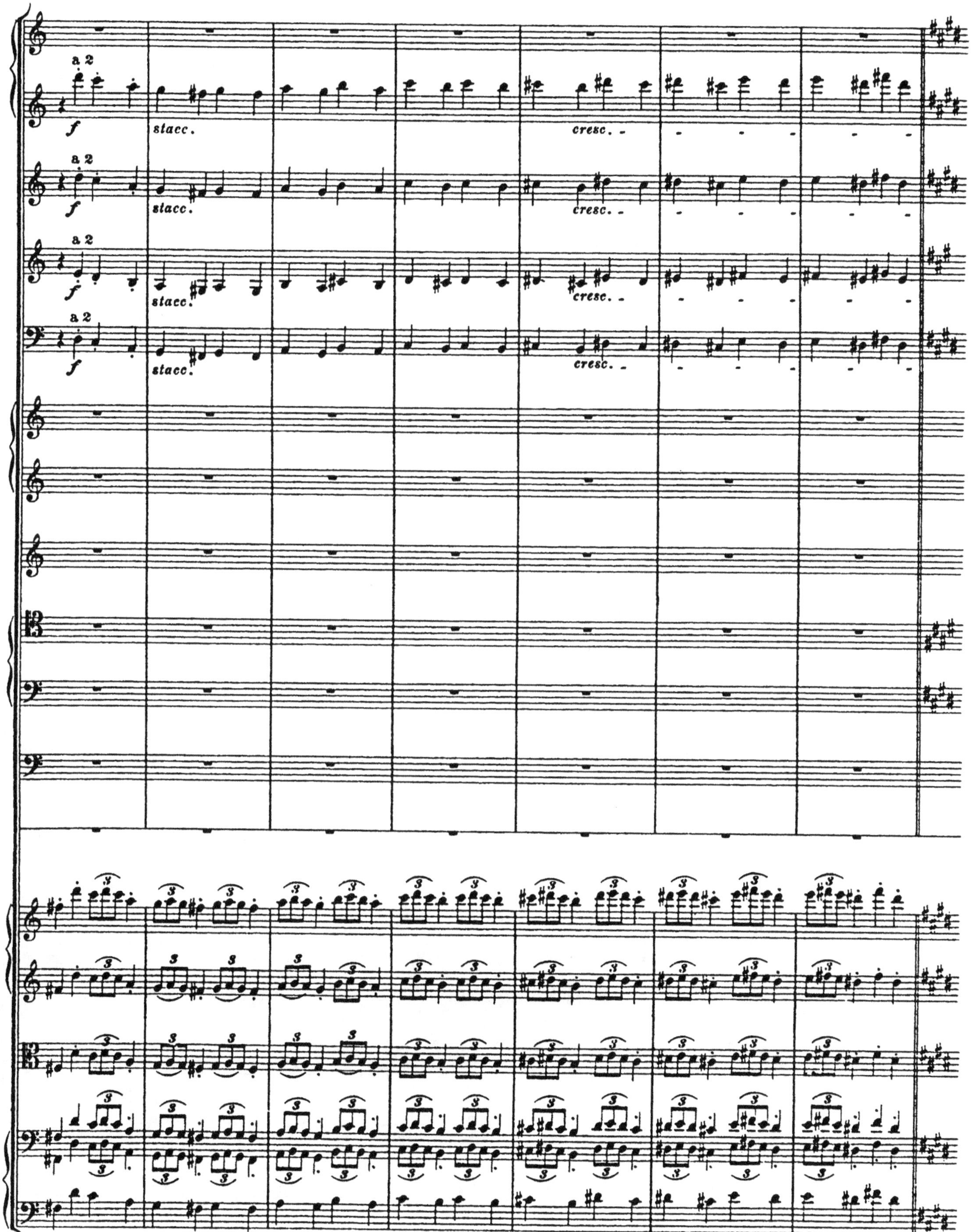

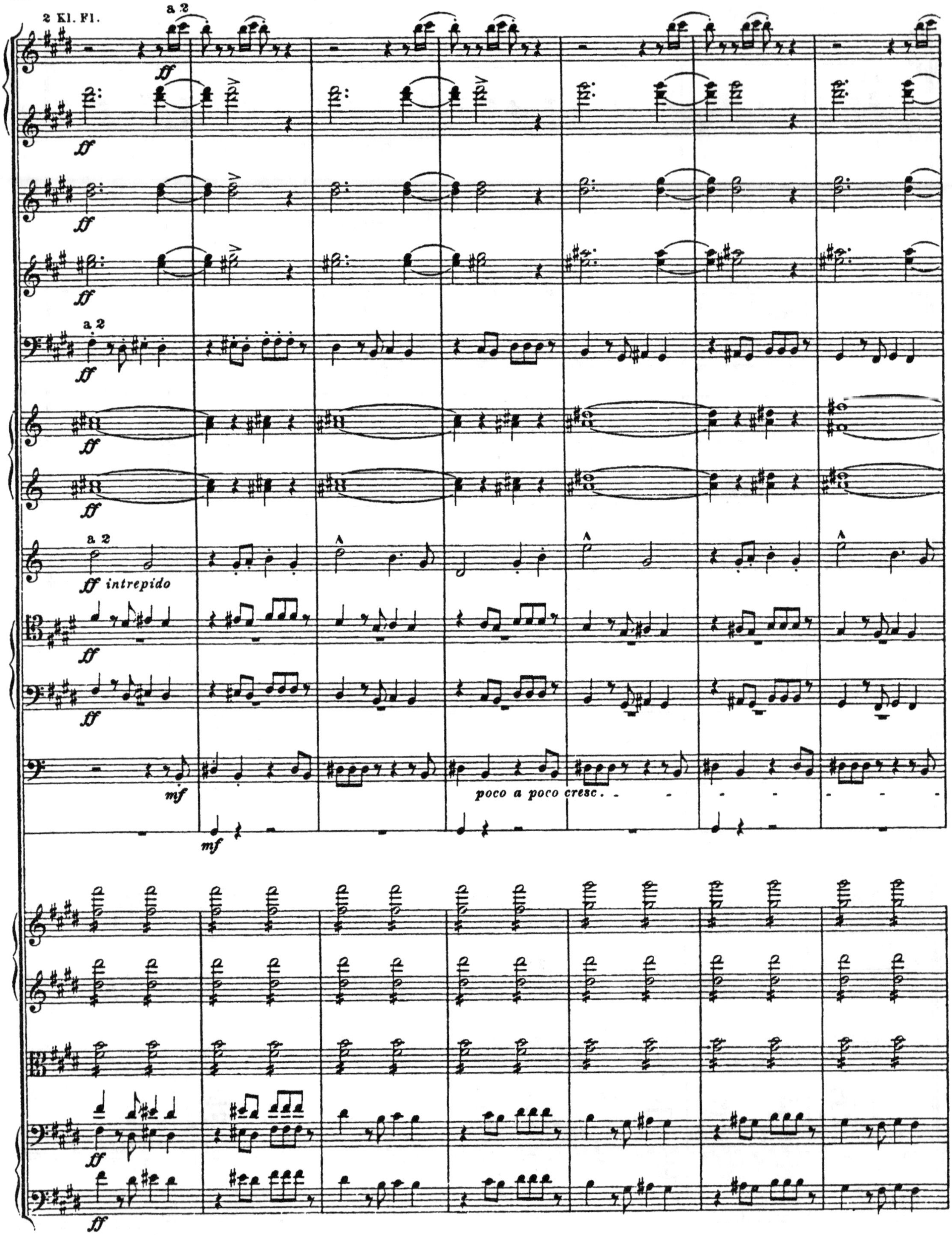
2 Kl. Fl.
a 2
ff
a 2
ff intrepido
mf
poco a poco cresc.

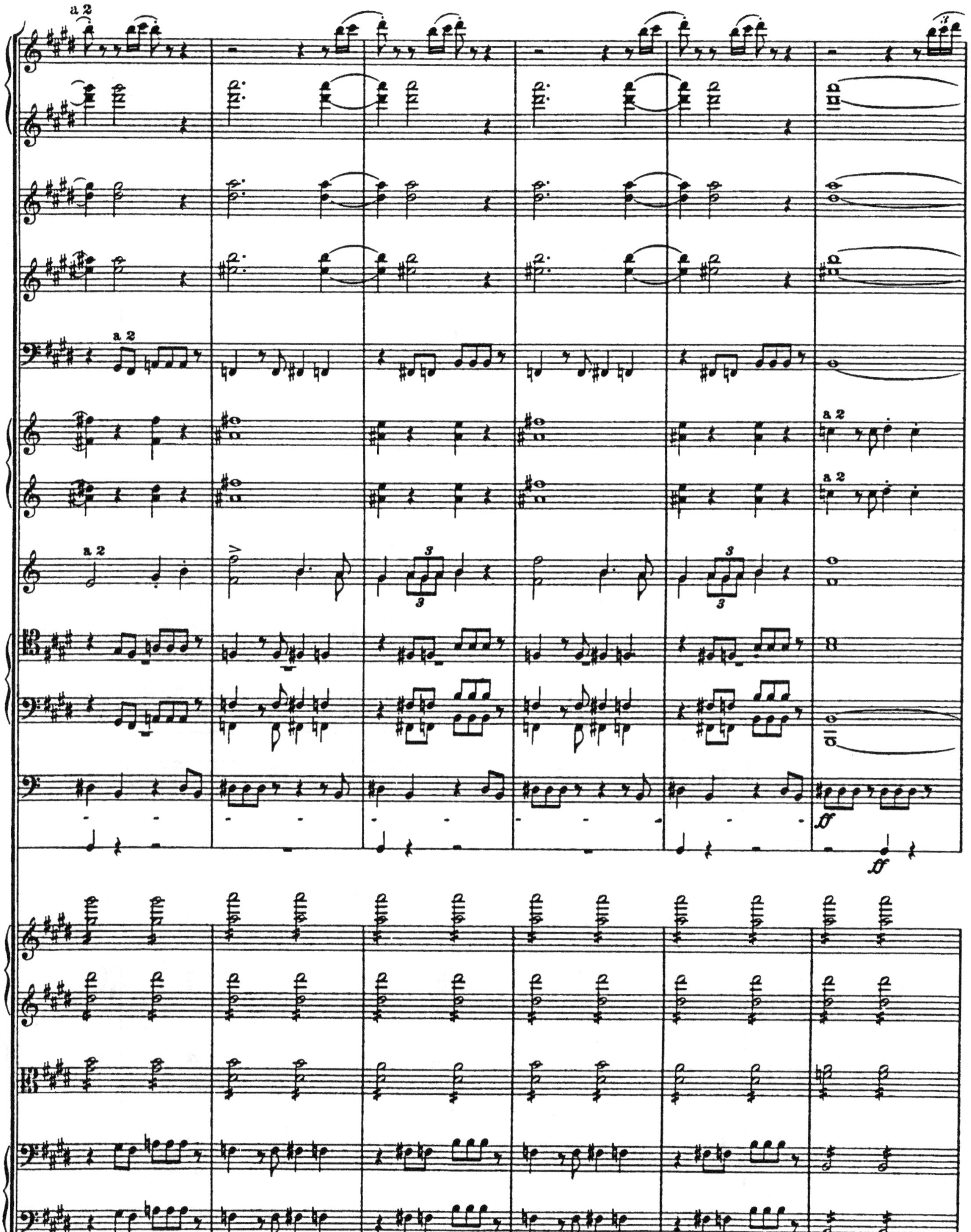
a 2
a 2
a 2
a 2
a 2
ff
ff

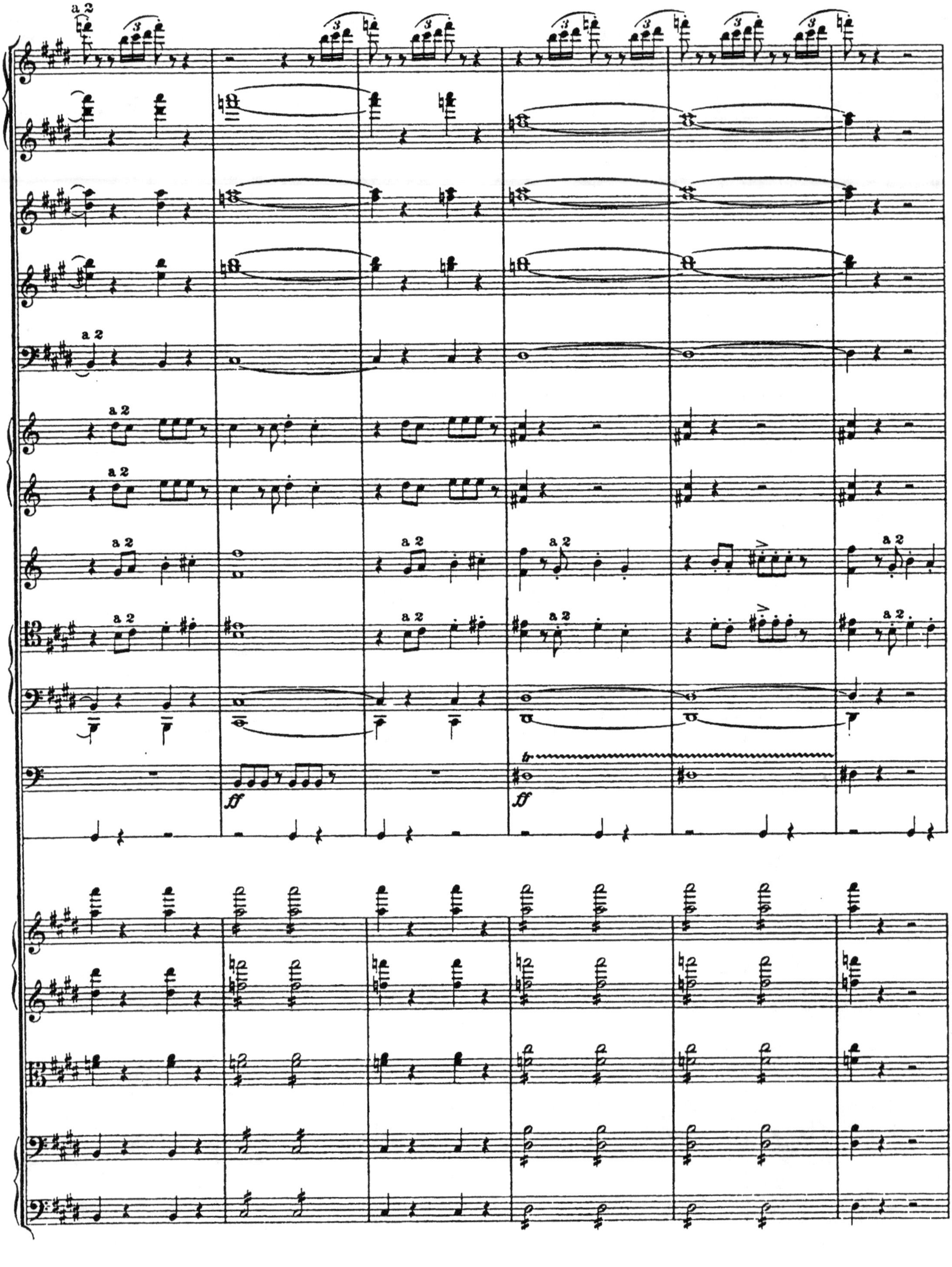
a 2
3
tr
ff

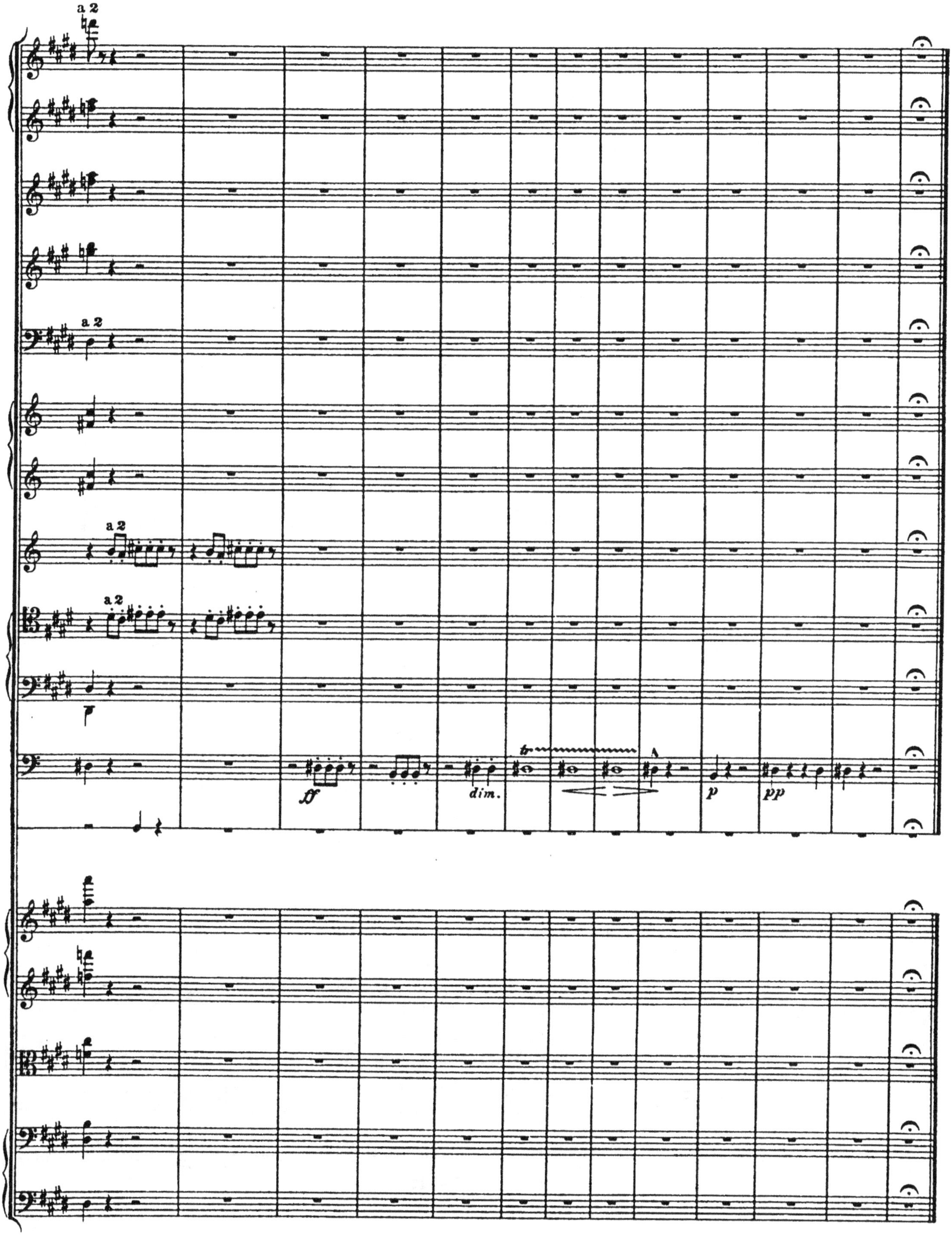
a 2
a 2
a 2
a 2
ff
dim.
p
pp

III.

Zum Grabe: Die Wiege des zukünftigen Lebens.

To the grave: The cradle of the future life.   À la tombe: berceau de la vie future.

A sírhoz: A tulvilági élet bölcsője.

Engl. Hr.
Klar.
Fag.
mf dolente
(f)
rinforz. espressivo dolente assai
arco
pizz.
sempre f
Engl. Hr.
Klar.
muta in C.
p
Vcl. u. Kb.

Fl.
(dolce)
Hob.
(dolce)
tr
sempre dolce
dolce
arco
dolce
Fl.
sempre dolce e legato
tr
sempre legato
sempre legato
Hob.
Klar. in C.
pp
Fag.
M. 68 =
pp
dolce cantando
pp
pp
pp
trem.
pp
trem.
pp
M. 68 =

Fl.
Hob.
Klar.
Fag.
sempre dolce e legato
espress.
con sordini
div.
(p)
sempre legato
con sord.
trem.
(pp)
Solo
con sordino
(p)
Tutti
con sord.
trem.
(pp)
Fl.
Hob.
Klar.
Fag.
Hr.
pp legato
pp
sost.
p
pp legato
Vcl.
Kb.
pp legato
pp legato
p

Hob.
Klar.
Fag.
Hr.
p
Hob.
Klar.
Fag.
Hr.
Tr.
Pk.
mf
mf un poco marc.
a 2
mf espress.
muta in E.
marc.
tr

Hob.
a2
Klar.
muta in A.
Fag.
Tr.
Pk.
pizz.
arco
p
pp
Fl.
Hob.
Klar.
in A.
Fag.
dolce
arco
p
pp

Fl.
Hob.
Klar.
Hr. 1. u. 2. in E.
pp
sempre pp
p un poco marc.
p dolciss.
perdendo

REVISIONSBERICHT

Nr. 1. Der nächtliche Zug.

Als Vorlage diente die gedruckte Partitur, erschienen bei J. Schuberth & Cie. 1862. Verlagsnummer 2791.

Zur Vergleichung war mir zugänglich eine Abschrift von Karl Götze mit Korrekturen von Liszt. Sie trägt das Datum 2. Mai 1861 und den Vermerk: Stichvorlage. Ferner eine gedruckte Partitur mit Korrekturen von Liszt vom Juni 1874.

Beide Partituren befinden sich im Lisztmuseum zu Weimar. Die darin enthaltene Vorschrift betreffs der Widmung an Carl Tausig und des Eindruckens von Teilen des Gedichtes in die Partitur wurde befolgt.

Seite 4 stand in der geschriebenen Partitur von unbekannter Hand neben der Vorschrift ›a tempo. Äußerst ruhig‹ die Bemerkung: ›Von hier an ein wenig bewegter‹. Diese wurde auch damals in die gedruckte Partitur aufgenommen, fehlt aber in der späteren Klavierübertragung.

Da der Meister selbst diese Stelle in verklärter Ruhe spielte, im Gegensatze zu dem fließenden Tempo, welches er stets beim Andante forderte, so glaubte ich mich berechtigt, die Bezeichnung ›äußerst ruhig‹ als eine eindringliche Mahnung, hier das Tempo nicht zu beschleunigen, allein bestehen zu lassen.

Seite 7 ›Un poco accelerando‹; Seite 12 ›agitato molto‹ und Seite 13 ›stringendo‹ sind der Klavierübertragung entnommen.

Nr. 2. Der Tanz in der Dorfschenke (Erster Mephisto-Walzer).

Material wie oben.

München, Mai 1913.

Die Bemerkung unter NB: ›Das Stück ist fast durchgängig im Vierviertel-Takt zu dirigieren‹ stammt von Liszt. Sie kann selbstverständlich nicht wörtlich befolgt werden, sondern es ist darunter ein viertaktiger Rhythmus zu verstehen.

Die Tempoangaben Seite 30 ›un poco meno mosso e rubato‹; Seite 33 ›vivace fantastico‹ stammen aus der Klavierübertragung.

Nr. 3. Zweiter Mephisto-Walzer.

Vorlage: Gedruckte Partitur, erschienen bei Ad. Fürstner. Verlagsnummer 2176.

Seite 2, 6. Takt steht in der Vorlage 1. Viol. drittes Sechzehntel, *d*. In der Klavierstimme dagegen *dis*.

Da ich diese Stelle beim Meister in letzterer Fassung gespielt habe und nicht anzunehmen ist, daß er sie im Orchester geändert haben wollte, entschied ich mich für *dis*.

Mehrere Vortragsbezeichnungen entstammen der Ausgabe für Klavier.

Nr. 4. Von der Wiege bis zum Grabe.

Vorlage: Gedruckte Partitur. Verlag Ed. Bote & G. Bock Nr. 12812. Erschienen 1883.

Zum Vergleiche lag vor die Ausgabe für Klavier und eine Instrumentierung der beiden letzten Teile (Manuskript aus dem Liszt-Museum in Weimar).

Die Ergänzungen der vielfach mangelnden Vortragsbezeichnungen sind dem Manuskript und der Klavierausgabe entnommen.

Berthold Kellermann